Daily Meditations

Flowing Tides

by Norman R. Perry

HUGHES & COLEMAN

NORWICH

"Hope thou in God..."

Psalm 42 v 5

A new day! A new month! How do we approach it? Some folk approach anything new with hope and expectation. Others seem to anticipate coming days with a certain measure of apprehension. This is sometimes explained by natural temperament, or by the fact that the future, as far as can be seen, is gloomy.

There are, though, other explanations, such as, a low view of God, a lack of faith, or too much dependence on other people. What about you today? Try to think afresh that the power, the wisdom and the grace of God, are still completely adequate to meet every need that can possibly arise.

It will not do to give credence to any suggestion that this day, or this month, will find that God is unable to guide and sustain. Approach this day, this month, with hope.

2nd Day   **A Safe Guide**

> *"He will guide you..."*
>
> John 16 v 13

Do you try to canalise the Spirit of God? Do you think He must go your way, and do your bidding? I am sure you do not consciously and deliberately do this, but there is always the danger of doing it subconsciously. Jesus said that God would give the Holy Spirit to them that ask Him.

It must never be forgotten though, that when the Spirit comes, He comes to direct, not to be directed, to comfort, not to be comforted, to rebuke, not to be rebuked.

The question is asked in the prophecy of Isaiah, "Who has directed the Spirit of the Lord, or being His Counsellor, has taught Him?" You and I must ever remember that the Spirit always guides wisely. He can do no other, for He is the Spirit of wisdom. Trust Him. He does not need your help.

3rd Day **Clear Vision**

"He...looked out at a window."

Genesis 26 v 8

Windows are most necessary and useful. We all have them in the place where we live. They enable us to see what is going on outside, as well as letting light into our rooms. Sometimes, however, the windows are not as clear as they might be, and we may tend to complain about impaired visibility.

But there is no real point in complaining that we cannot see out of the window if the dirt is on the inside where we can clean it off ourselves.

Such things as envy, anger, jealousy, resentment, cynicism and bitterness, all tend to cloud the inside of the windows of our hearts and minds. This results in an outlook on the outside world which will be false and distorted. Seek grace to keep the inside of your spiritual windows clear. Things will look much healthier.

4th Day   **Hide and Seek**

"Woe to them that seek deep to hide
their counsel from the Lord."

Isaiah 29 v 15

To attempt to hide anything from God is to try to do something which is doomed to failure from the start. Earnestly to seek something from God, is sure to result in success. By this, I do not mean that we shall of necessity receive exactly what we ask for, but of this we can be certain, God will not give us something inferior.

The wise man heeds the word which says, "Seek earnestly the best gifts", and we must leave it to Him to know what are the best gifts for us. As to hiding, we must not try to hide anything from Him, for the Bible declares, "there is nothing hidden which shall not be revealed". Rather then, confess what we might prefer to hide, for He alone can effectively and finally hide these things – even our sin – under the atoning blood.

"...He knoweth the way that I take..."
Job 23 v 10

When the above words were spoken, the speaker was in deep trouble. His whole world had collapsed around him, his friends failed to understand him and often imputed wrong motives and actions to him. This, understandably, added to his trouble.

Although Job lived a long time ago, and resided in a far-off land, we know that there are still many people who find themselves in terrible trouble today. Such folk can well understand Job's feelings and his expressions, and possibly you find yourself in some such situation. To anyone in such trouble, words seem poor indeed. Yet it is still true that while

I may not know the way He goes;
I rest in this, my way He knows.

This was Job's comfort and confidence; God grant that it may be ours.

6th Day   **Possessions**

"A man's life consists not in the abundance
of the things which he possesses"

Luke 12 v 15

Possessions by themselves do not bring happiness. I remember once reading some words by one of the world's richest men. He said, "My riches have been my greatest burden". Yet so many people seem to think that if only they had more money or goods, they would automatically be more contented. This is not necessarily so.

It has often been observed that the larger the garden or field, the more weeds there are likely to be. This is an age of striving to obtain more and more of this world's goods. Let me quote Proverbs 13 v 7 "One man pretends to be rich, yet has nothing; another pretends to be poor, yet has great wealth."

The man who has God for his Father, Jesus Christ as His Saviour, and the Holy Spirit as His Guide, is rich above all computing.

7th Day   **Disappointments**

"Without counsel, purposes are disappointed..."
Proverbs 15 v 22

There is not one of us who has not known disappointment. In fact, we have probably known many disappointments in the course of our lives. It would be a strange thing if we were to go for any length of time without being disappointed about something.

Possibly, even now, you are smarting under the failure of some cherished ambition, or may be you are feeling a great sense of disappointment because of the behaviour of some person in whom you had put your trust.

There are just two things I would like to say to you. The first is that this disappointment may well have been allowed because God has appointed something better for you, which you have not as yet seen. The second thing is, God will never be a disappointment to you. His counsel will determine the carrying out of His gracious appointments for you.

"His disciples...went and told Jesus."
Matthew 14 v 12

There are some things which we cannot share with other people. Secret and private hopes and fears, ambitions and disappointments, joys and sorrows, some of these we cannot tell to any other person. Sometimes, too, there appears to be no way of deliverance open to us. What then is to be done? Luther once wrote,

"Bear and forbear and silent be,
Tell to no man thy misery,
Yield not in trouble to despair,
God can deliver any day."

This means that, like the disciples in past days, we always have a friend to whom we can go, one who will never turn us away. More that this, He will listen with a most sympathetic ear to what we have to say, and will fully understand, and help wisely and lovingly.

"A perfect and an upright man"

Job 1 v 8

What a tremendously difficult thing it is to make a completely honest assessment of ourselves. Some of us may be given to self-deprecation, while others may tend to words of self-praise. The problem is we cannot see ourselves as we really are. This means that not one of us can appreciate how we appear to others. Further, we learn from Scripture that we have deceitful hearts, and this makes true self-analysis impossible.

Only God is in a position to assess us with absolute accuracy, and this He has done in His declaration that "There is none righteous, no, not one". For acceptance with God, we must, like Job, look for help outside ourselves.

Job said, "I know that my Redeemer liveth". The redeemed have Christ's righteousness upon them, and are then assessed by God and accounted perfect.

10th Day   **Clinical or Compassionate**

"...The Son of God who loved me..."
Galatians 2 v 20

What a difference there is in people in their way of speaking, and in the manner of their doing things! Doctors and nurses are essential and highly valuable members of any community. Yet how they can differ.

There are some who are highly efficient, they know their job well, and do it in a most capable way. There is though, a coldly clinical approach, which some find almost chilling. Others equally skilled, seem to radiate warmth and feeling as they work.

Think of Jesus Christ, and the way He did His healing work. Never was He cold or clinical. Always He revealed Himself as one who saw His patients as people who needed love as well as skilled care. This He always gave. This He still gives.

"...and the princes...saw these men, upon
whose bodies the fire had no power..."
Daniel 3 v 27

When the three Hebrew children refused to bow down before the image set up by the mighty Nebuchadnezzar, they seemed doomed. There appeared to be no possibility of any deliverance. After all, who was there capable of dealing with such a despotic ruler? A dreadful end seemed to be certain.

Yet here is another illustration of a deliverance being effected without threats, weapons or an army. The fiery furnace was made seven times hotter than was usual, but it had no power on these men. What was the reason? How could it be explained? The answer can be found in Isaiah 43 v 2 "When thou passest through the waters, I will be with thee...when thou walkest through the fire, thou shalt not be burned".

God said, "I will be with thee" – and He was! For in the furnace is seen "the form of the fourth" – the Son of God, keeping His word.

12th Day   **What's the Time?**

"...the times and the seasons..."

Acts 1 v 7

I daresay you have often been asked the time by children, but have you noticed that they nearly always ask, "Please could you tell me the right time?" Near enough, seems not good enough. When we come to think of it, we shall surely see it is important that we should be concerned with time. One fact that immediately emerges, is that we have no control over it. Rather, we are governed by it.

Again, we are limited by it. Frequently, too, people say, "I have no time to spare". But there are some things that cry out for our thoughtful consideration. The prophet Hosea had to tell Israel, "It is time to seek the Lord". Isaiah said, "Seek ye the Lord while He may be found". This clearly implies that there will be a time when He will not be found. Have we sought Him? We desperately need Him – NOW!

13th Day   **Holy Service**

"...His servants shall serve Him..."
Revelation 22 v 3

There are many kinds of service; there is military service, civil service, social service, domestic service, voluntary service and a host of other forms of service. But I am reminded of the Psalmist who, in Psalm 84 v 10 declares, "I had rather be a door-keeper in the house of my God, than to dwell in the tents of wickedness".

Here indeed, is what appears to be a very lowly service but, in reality, is a high and honourable post. In fact, to be engaged in any form of service for the Lord is a high honour.

To serve God in any capacity, is to be engaged in a holy and happy task which will never cease. God's service entered upon here on earth, will be continued in heaven. Never does it become drudgery, but it is an occupation which gives increasing delight. So, serve the Lord with gladness.

14th Day   **Useless Pretence**

"Come in, thou wife of Jeroboam; why feignest thou thyself to be another?"

I Kings 14 v 6

King Jeroboam built an altar in Bethel and departed from the ways of the Lord by making two golden calves to worship there. God gave Jeroboam a severe warning but he did not change his evil and idolatrous ways.

When his son became ill, Jeroboam instructed his wife to disguise herself and call on the prophet Ahijah to discover from him whether his son would recover. Now Ahijah had lost his sight but God had given him to know that the wife of the king was coming and was pretending to be someone else. Ahijah was not deceived and gave the king's wife a solemn message of God's judgement on Jeroboam and his family because of his evil ways.

When God's children are in touch with Him they need not be deceived but will be given God's Word to answer those who are opposed to their Lord.

"A message from God..."

Judges 3 v 20

Nothing is more annoying to some people than to pick up a newspaper, read a few items, and then suddenly realise that it is not the current issue. With what disgust they throw it down, exclaiming, "This is yesterday's paper!" I expect we all know the feeling. We all like news which is up-to-date.

Have you ever realised that there is some news which is not, and never will be, out of date? This news is of the greatest importance to you and to me. Its importance lies in the fact that it has to do with this world and the next, and it is found in the Bible.

If you desire to know about life and death, sin and salvation, joy and peace, read the Bible – God's Word to you. It has a message for you today.

16th Day   **What Does It Mean?**

"What mean ye by this...?"
Exodus 12 v 26

How many times have we been puzzled by some statement or happening – something which we could not explain. We turn it over and over in our minds, and the more we think about it, the less we understand it. Such things tend to recur to our minds, and can become quite an annoyance.

There may even now be something like this affecting you in your life. It is possible to get quite upset by such experiences, yet there may very well be no real reason for concern at all.

If only we could remember that God knows all about it and leave it with Him, what peace of heart and mind it would bring. Should you just now be agitated by something like this, "Take it to the Lord in prayer". He will know how to deal with it.

17th Day   **Clouds and Sun**

"I will cover the sun with a cloud."
Ezekiel 32 v 7

If you laze in the sun, the cloud will annoy,
If you toil in the heat, the cloud will bring joy.

The holiday-maker usually looks for, and enjoys
the bright sunny days, when it is comfortable to
lie about and relax. For him to see clouds rising,
can be a source of disappointment, and even
anger. But the labourer, toiling in the burning
heat, finds the shadow of a cloud a most welcome
relief. We see then, how very different people's
reactions are to the same happening.

How true this is in our daily lives in almost all
circumstances. What pleases us, may well
aggravate other people. Let us then face the fact
that it is far better that God should send cloud
and sunshine as He sees fit, rather than leave the
control to us, which would end in complete
disaster.

18th Day   **Steady Now**

"Tarry ye until..."

Luke 24 v 49

The disciples of Jesus had spent some three years listening to, and watching Him. As a result, they knew a great deal about Him, and the method of His working. Yet knowledge, excellent though it is, may not be sufficient of itself.

The Lord had a definite purpose for them, but they had to wait for a little while before they commenced the work He intended them to do. What they lacked was power. Often, too, it is like this with us. We do so eagerly desire to get on with things for which we may think we are fit and ready.

God, however, may see there is something else we need to learn, and this is the reason why we are kept waiting. It is always better to wait for Him, than to hurry on without proper preparation. So, wait patiently.

19th Day   **Perfectly Matched**

"God saw that it was good."
Genesis 1 v 25

I have often been impressed by the fact that in nature, the shade of green seen in the leaves of a plant always tones in with the colour of the flowers. Or, put it the other way round, the colour of the flowers and the shade of the leaves never clash.

When we think of the extraordinary number of shades of green there are, this lack of clashing is most remarkable. If we try to match up some flowers with other leaves, we often find that the two do not go together.

Surely there is a lesson here for us. If God wonderfully and unfailingly matches leaves with flowers, we can surely trust Him to blend the events which make up our lives. When we are able to see things as God sees them, we shall realise that there is a perfect blending of prosperity and adversity, of light and shade, of joy and sorrow.

20th Day   **Sleeping and Waking**

"Jacob awaked out of his sleep"
Genesis 28 v 16

Sleep is both a necessity and a mystery. It is a kind of suspended animation. It is estimated that we spend a third of our lives sleeping. Restful sleep is indeed a great blessing for which we ought to be very grateful. During sleep, our minds and bodies are rested and refreshed, to fit us for the waking hours.

What is so necessary, is for us to strike a right balance between wakefulness and sleep. On one occasion, Christ said to His disciples, "Sleep on now and take your rest." To others, Paul said, "It is high time to awake out of sleep". Happy are they who serve God during their waking hours, and sleep peacefully at night.

Let us always recognise and acknowledge that we are dependent on Him for power to serve, and for ability to sleep, and He knows our needs.

"Summer and winter shall not cease."

Genesis 8 v 22

November, damp and cold seems far removed from the sun and warmth of June. Every year contains a November and a June, with many variations in between. Summer and winter are ordinances of God which will continue until the end of time, because He has promised it.

In the life of the Christian too, there are seasons. At times, we are full of the joy of the Lord, and it seems like high summer. At other times, the whole outlook seems bleak, and it feels like winter in the soul.

So it must be while we are in this world. There will be the changing seasons in the soul's experience, some bright and joyful, some dull and sad. But this will only be for a little while. There will be no dreary, dismal seasons in heaven. So, lift up your heart, the best is yet to be.

22nd Day   **Humble Instruments**

"...God prepared a worm..."

Jonah 4 v 7

A worm! Yes, a humble worm! Can you read these words in the Book of Jonah and then believe that God can not find some use for you? If you are a Christian, then there is something, however insignificant it may be in your eyes, that you can do, and remember it is a great privilege to be used by Him in any capacity. The account of Jonah's experience is very illuminating, for we read there, amongst other things, that God prepared a great fish, a worm, a gourd and an east wind. How dare we then imagine that there is no task for us? It is difficult to think of a more striking contrast than a great fish and a worm. God used both. Ask Him to use you. You may get a surprise.

"Himself took our infirmities..."
Matthew 8 v 17

"I didn't want to get mixed up with it." How often have we heard words like this! They indicate an unwillingness to get involved in a certain matter. Now of course, there are some things it is right and wise to keep out of. There are also other matters in which we ought to become involved.

You will recall that the priest and the Levite in Christ's parable did not desire to get involved with the wounded man by the roadside. The Samaritan stopped and helped him.

Ought we to get involved in something today? Somebody may need our help, and if so, let us not keep out of helping them. Think again of how the Saviour involved Himself closely and painfully with us, and what our position would have been if He had "passed by on the other side".

"Be renewed in the spirit of your mind."
Ephesians 4 v 23

What a marvellous thing the mind is, and what a difference there is in people's minds! Of some we say, "They are strong-minded", of others, "they are weak-minded", and we well know that some are very absent-minded.

Some years ago, I remember reading something by an ancient writer. He wrote, "To be familiar with great minds, will help to shape some greatness in our own". Doubtless, there is some truth in this statement. It is probably true that those we associate with affect our thought patterns too.

Sadly though, we must not forget that our minds have been adversely affected by the fall, so that Romans 8 v 7 declares, "The carnal mind is enmity against God . . ." Over against this, the Christian is in a happy position, for of believers Paul says, "We have the mind of Christ". Is this true of you?

*"All things work together for good to them
that love God."*

Romans 8 v 28

Nothing has ever happened, nothing is
happening now, and nothing will ever happen to
those who love God, that is not for their good.
This is a tremendously sweeping statement to
make, but it is surely justified by the quotation
standing at the top of this page.

When we are passing through a period in our
lives when everything appears to be going wrong,
it is a helpful exercise to consider whether
Romans 8 v 28 really means what it says. If it
does, then whatever the appearance of things –
and they may seem to be against us – the reality is
that actually, strangely and mysteriously, they
are all working together for our good. Why is
this? It is because God is in supreme control of all
that concerns those that love Him, and of all
other things, too.

26th Day   **Growth**

"Consider the lilies of the field, how they grow."
Matthew 6 v 28

Growth is a most mysterious process. Its secret, like the secret of life itself, belongs to God. But, before there can be growth, there must be life. This is true in the spiritual and in the natural realms. If we have not been born again by the power of the Holy Spirit, we are not even Christians. We may call ourselves such, but it is not bearing the name of Christian that makes us Christians. It is having the new nature. As Jesus said, "You must be born again".

It will be seen at once, that if we have not this new life, we are still in the same condition as when we were born "dead in sins". Therefore there cannot be growth in any spiritual sense until we are born again of the Spirit of God. Are you truly born again of the Spirit? Are you growing in grace?

27th Day   **Fruit Bearing**

"Behold, the husbandman waiteth for the precious fruit."

James 5 v 7

Yesterday we were thinking of growth. One of the great purposes of growth is to produce fruit. This is the purpose of planting orchards – not merely that there may be a great show of leaves, or even a beautiful mass of blossom. These things are indeed good to look at, but they are not the main purpose of an orchard!

Jesus made very clear statements to the disciples about fruit-bearing. In John's Gospel, chapter 15 v 16, He says, "I have chosen you...that you should go and bring forth fruit, and that your fruit should remain".

If indeed, we are true believers, we are branches of the true vine – Jesus Christ. It is only as we abide in Him, and draw our sustenance from Him, that we shall bring forth fruit to His glory – good fruit – in abundance.

28th Day   **Please Explain**

"He expounded all things to His disciples."
Mark 4 v 34

Many years ago I attended a service in a small country chapel. After the singing of the first hymn, a lady sitting next to me offered me a book, saying "Would you like this?" It was a tune book. I still wonder why she offered it to me. Was it that she hoped I might sing tenor, or bass? Or – was it perhaps that she hoped I might sing the tune! At any rate, her action still leaves me puzzled.

Is it not a fact that people often say or do things which we cannot understand? It may be that they imagine that we know what they mean, without any further explanation.

The disciples of Christ did not always grasp the meaning of some of His words and actions. Then they asked Him to explain. He often graciously acceded to their request. He still does!

Ask Him.

"Why hast Thou thus dealt with us?"

Luke 2 v 48

Surely there is not one of us who has not asked the question, "Why?" Sometimes it has been an anxious enquiry, sometimes mere curiosity. The question is asked in times of stress, such as bereavement, pain, weakness, disappointment, and, of course, in many other circumstances.

Such a query indicates ignorance – an inability to find satisfying answers to life's troubles. What so often happens then, is that we may feel that there is no real answer to, or reason for, the trials and problems of life. Such a conclusion must be wrong.

In daily life, children are always asking "Why?" because they believe their parents know the answer. Parents, however, do not always know all the answers. God's children are in a vastly different situation. Their Father does know the answers. So, seek to drop that nagging "Why?", and leave Him to explain in His own good time.

"Seek ye first the Kingdom of God, and His righteousness..."

Matthew 6 v 33

Christ's words quoted above were spoken to His followers, and like all His utterances, were intended to be taken seriously. They illustrate the sad fact that we who profess to be His disciples often set our hearts and minds on things other than the Kingdom of God. This diligent seeking of God's Kingdom, Christ urges as a first priority.

We, unhappily, in practice, if not intentionally in desire, put it much lower down the list. First things first, is a most excellent motto for Christians to follow, and the Lord shows us here what should be first. In saying this, however, He does not overlook the fact that in this life we need other things as well.

These, I suggest, come as a bonus to all who seek God's Kingdom first, because Jesus continues, "and all these things shall be added unto you". What a bonus!

31st Day   **Hopes and Fears**

"Why art thou disquieted?...hope in God..."
Psalm 42 v 5

This is the last entry in this booklet. It means that another month of thirty-one days has ended. What varied experiences can be crowded into the short space of a month. You have doubtless had your hopes and fears, and many other feelings as well. Sometimes our worst fears are realised, and sometimes our highest hopes are fulfilled. Both are necessary.

A writer of many years ago put it like this, "Hope is like the cork to the net, which keeps the soul from sinking in despair, and fear is like the lead to the net, which keeps it from floating in presumption".

The net needs to go down into the dark depths, which can represent the place of fear, that it may rise again with a harvest of fish.

"Hopes and fears alternate rise."

But fear will ultimately vanish, and hope will triumph, for God is faithful.